GARY JONES

Riga

This book was professionally typeset on Reedsy.
Find out more at reedsy.com

Contents

Introduction   iv

Brief History and Background   1

Best Time to Go and Weather   6

Transportation to and From Riga   11

Top 5 Affordable Hotels   19

Top Restaurants   25

Best Famous Landmarks in the City   32

Best Museums, Theatres and Art Galleries   41

Best Coffee Shops   50

Top Bars and Night Clubs   56

Special Things You Can Only Do in Riga   62

3 Days in Riga – Travel Itinerary   74

Conclusion   91

Thank You   92

Introduction

Riga, Latvia belongs to the European Union that's often forgotten, but definitely worth a visit. While the country is definitely gaining popularity among tourists, the amount of visitors is not yet so excessive as to make it difficult for you to walk around and explore its beauty. This is why if you're thinking about vacationing anywhere nice – Riga should definitely be on the list, allowing you to become one of the privileged few to visit.

But what exactly can you find there? In this book, you'll find out exactly what Riga, Latvia has to offer during your stay there. Know what bars, nightclubs, restaurants, and tourist locations you should check out in order to get a full feel of the country. By the end of this book, you can easily create an itinerary for yourself during a stay in Riga, whether you're only there for a day, three days, or even a full week.

1

Brief History and Background

When considering a vacation somewhere in the Baltic States, few people think about Latvia first, so you're actually one of the few lucky enough to consider this country as a vacation spot. The largest city in Latvia is Riga, which is also the largest city in the three Baltic States.

Before we talk about Riga however, it's important to first talk about the country of Latvia and what you can expect from this quietly upscale place.

Latvia enjoys its independence nowadays since it was under Soviet occupation from 1940 to 1991. Hence, the independence of Latvia is fairly new, relatively speaking, as it regained its independence only in 1991.

During Soviet occupation, many Russians moved to Latvia but upon the country's independence, these very same Russians were not automatically granted Latvian citizenship because they migrated during the Soviet occupation. Today, the Russian population in the city is steadily declining as Latvian citizens regain control of the country.

City of Riga

Founded in 1201, the historical center of Riga is actually a UNESCO World Heritage Site. The city was known as the European Capital of Culture and welcomed more than 1.4 million visitors, made possible by the Riga International Airport.

There are currently 639,630 people living in Riga, the number actually declining since 1991 when it had more than 900,000 inhabitants. The reason for this is a combination of emigration as well as low birth rates in the area.

2

Best Time to Go and Weather

The best time to visit Riga would depend on what you actually want to see while on vacation. The climate is typically defined as humid continental, which means that even the summer is fairly cool, with temperatures ranging around 18 degrees Celsius to 30 degrees Celsius. The colder months will give you a temperature of anywhere from -20 to -25 degrees Celsius. Since it's so close to the sea, autumn rain and fogs are to be expected on a routine basis.

So when should you actually go?

- If you want to avoid the teeming crowd, the best time to go is January. It's actually one of the colder months – which is why there's few people milling about in the area. The good thing about this is that you can enjoy most of the sights and activities without having to fight for it with the other tourists. The downside is of course – you're going to be freezing the whole time.

· If you want good weather while still avoiding the crowd, come in May or July. June is the peak season in the city, which means that if you visit in June, you'll be banging shoulders with a lot of people. During the early weeks of May however, the tourists shouldn't be all in yet and by July, many of them have left already. The climate during this time is relatively warm so you'll be able to enjoy many of the activities.

- If you want to visit Latvia on a budget, you should probably visit around February or March. Again, these would be the colder months – but the temperature should be getting close to comfortable. During these months, hotel rooms can go for as low as $35 per night – making it remarkably cheaper than the $110 you'll have to pay during the month of May.

· If what you're after is warm weather, then check in during the months of June, July, August, and September. If you'll notice though, these are also the peak season months so expect a little bit of competition for transport, sights, and hotel rooms.

Keep the weather in mind and pack accordingly!

3

Transportation to and From Riga

Despite the fact that it's not exactly a high publicized tourist destination, Riga is wonderfully easy to access from various major points. To start off, there's the International Airport which will be touched on in a moment. The city in itself is home to several national roads such as the Europe Route E22 and the Via Baltica, which will be discussed later on as well.

So you basically have three ways to get to Riga: by plane, by sea, and by land.

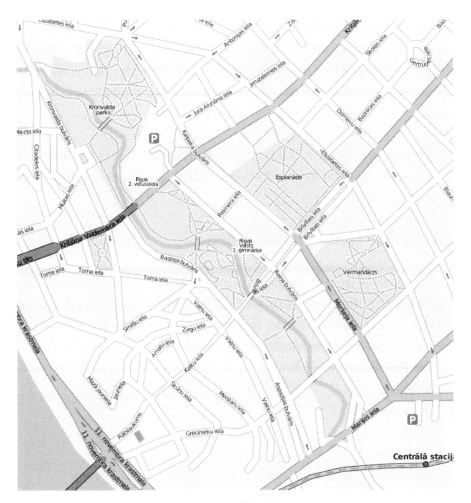

Old Town Riga Map

(© OpenStreetMap contributors)

Through Riga International Airport

There's only one active airport in Riga, but it offers international flights. This should be perfect for those flying from overseas. The Riga International Airport with a code of RIX was built in 1973 but was continuously upgraded to meet the high standards required of international travel nowadays. This means that the airport is capable of accommodating large aircrafts including the Airbus A340, Boeing 747, 757, 767, and 777. This ability to accommodate numerous aircrafts means that Latvia is able to welcome as many as 4.7 million visitors per year.

Unfortunately, it can still be tough to find direct flights to Latvia, so you'll typically have to board several planes or connecting flights in order to get to the city.

International Coach Transport to Riga

You can also go to Riga via the Riga International Coach Terminal. The coach service offers both domestic and international connections and passes by several cities before reaching the main area of Latvia. Some of the places where the coach service stops are:
- St. Petersburg
- Prague
- London
- Berlin
- Stuttgart
- Rotterdam
- Talinn
- Minsk

The Bus companies that provide this service vary with schedules that cover all days of the week, giving you as much options as possible. Following are some of the bus companies you'd want to check out to find out if they run through your jump off point:

- TOKS P UAB
- EUROLINES
- Lux Express
- Vissa SIA
- Alma LTD SIA
- KAVTOK SIA
- **OLIMP SIA**

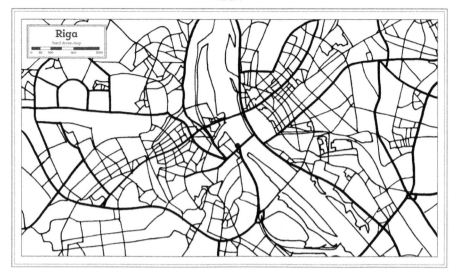

Public Transport around Riga

Public transport within the city is provided by just one supplier which is Rigas Satiksme.

There are trams, buses, and trolleybuses, covering a wide expanse of the city. As of 2012, there's also a minibus service. Within the country, you can use the national carrier Passenger Train.

4

Top 5 Affordable Hotels

So you arrived in Riga – what do you do next? Ideally, you already have a booking in one of the many hotels available in the city. If not however, you might want to check inside one of these affordable hotels, conveniently located within the city.

Radisson Blu Latvija Conference & Spa Hotel

Location: Elizabetes iela 55, Riga, LV-1010, Latvia
    Lowest Room Rate: 40 Euros

This 4-star hotel is located smack in the center of Riga and just 400m away from the Old Town. Rising high above the city, you get a beautiful bird's eye view of the sights below while at the same time enjoying all the comforts of home. The hotel boasts of spa facilities, dining venues, and even wireless internet connection. The rooms come with a mini bar, coffee making facilities, and all the modern amenities expected of a private bathroom.

You'll find that many of the best restaurants and bars in the area are located right within the walls of Radisson Blue. Hence, you really don't have to go far in order to sample the local cuisine or the thriving nightlife. If you're a solo traveler, Radisson Blu will give you an added layer of safety. There's also a wellness center, swimming pool, sauna, steam rooms, and spa treatments.

The hotel offers 24-desk staff and can provide added service such as luggage storage and currency exchange. Landmarks close by include the Freedom Monument, the Riga Train Station, and the Riga Airport.

Neiburgs Hotel

Location: Jauniela 25/27, Centra rajons, Rīga, LV-1050, Latvia
    Lowest Room Rate: 93 Euros

This 4-star hotel is beautifully located near the heart of the Old Town. It overlooks the Dome Square and comes with air-conditioned rooms plus a kitchenette in case you want to come with your own food. Calling it a room would be inaccurate though because accommodations are primarily like mini-apartments with their own wireless internet, DVD player, flat screen TV, and even a living area. If you happen to visit during the cold season, you'll love the bathroom floor heating that will keep you comfortable while enjoying their shower.

The front desk staff is available 24 hours a day – which is great as this lets you explore the Old Town for as long as you want. There's even a small in-house gym where you can sweat out some of the food you enjoyed or if you're particularly tired, there's the steam bath and sauna. For the readers, the hotel comes with a cozy but well-lit library. The hotel itself comes with a restaurant serving buffet breakfast, but feel free to explore a little more for lunch and dinner.

Close by the hotel are numerous landmarks including Central Railway Station and the Latvian National Opera. Since it's located in the heart of Riga, you'll have no problem walking around the area and exploring the Old Town on foot.

Radi Un Draugi

Location: Mārstaļu iela 3, Riga, LV-1050, Latvia
  Lowest Room Rate: 48 Euros

A 4-star hotel, the Radi Un Draugi is located near the Old Town and is just a few minutes away from famous landmarks. The rooms are equipped with air conditioning, beautifully complemented with warm colors and coffee making facilities. There's also a safe for your valuables, cable TV, and a modern bathroom. Some rooms come with refrigerators, but all of them have access to high speed wireless internet.

The desk staff is available on all hours of the day. Added facilities include luggage storage, concierge, and car rental. They also have an in-house restaurant serving all kinds of dishes, not to mention a sumptuous breakfast buffet packed with international and local dishes. The lounge room will welcome you after a tiring day walking through the Old Town. There's also a café bar where you can get cocktails – which means that you don't really have to go far.

On foot, you can easily reach the historic Dome Cathedral as well as get an excellent bird's eye view of the Old Town by visiting the St. Peter's Church, which is literally right by the corner. The Riga International Airport is also close by and the hotel also offers shuttle service.

Opera Hotel and Spa

Location: Raiņa bulvāris 33, Riga, LV-1050, Latvia
   Lowest Room Rate: 47 Euro

Just 5 minutes away from the Old Town of Riga, this beautiful piece of architecture deceptively hides a sleek modern interior with all the amenities of home. Each room comes with wireless internet, mini-bars, a safe, and a flat screen television while a select few come with whirlpool baths.

The rooms offer an amazing view of the Opera Park and the bridge spanning the River Daugava. The hotel itself is home to Boulevard 33, a famous restaurant serving organic food made into Latvian signature dishes plus international cuisine for those who want a taste of home while on foreign land. If you arrive during the summer, then you can take advantage of the terrace for your breakfast or just to relax in after a tour. The hotel also has 2 conference rooms, a spa, and a plunge pool.

Taking a walk outside, you'll find yourself just a few minutes away from the Latvian National Opera. There's also the main train station and the Riga International Airport 5 minutes away.

Tree House
   Location: Kaļķu iela 11a (4th floor), Riga, LV-1050, Latvia
   Lowest Room Rate: 34 Euro

The Tree House is a contemporary hotel that's primarily built for tourists traveling in groups. It's in the heart of Riga City with an interior décor that's meant to pop out in pictures. Pastel colors lining the walls and adorning the furniture, the room is further made comfortable with wireless internet and air conditioning. It's a dormitory type of accommodation, so expect the bathroom to be shared. There's also a shared kitchen with a toaster, an oven, and other kitchenware.

The Tree House comes with wireless internet connection throughout the property. The staff should be available at all times to give assistance in case you need something done.

Once you step outside, you're greeted by the sprawling streets of Riga with easy access to many of the landmarks and restaurants in the area. Close by is the Latvian National Opera and a wide expanse of greeneries to help you chill out with nature. Take a walk in the park and you'll encounter another famous landmark, which is the Freedom Monument.

Obviously, those aren't the only hotels in Riga, Latvia – but these are the top 5 rated ones when it comes to access, beauty, comfort, and prices. Whether you're traveling as part of a family, as a group, as a couple, or just by yourself – you should be able to find a hotel that fits within any of these 5 choices.

5

Top Restaurants

Riga is home to some of the most amazing chefs, heading world-class restaurants to soothe your palate. Whether you're looking for fine dining or something a little bit on the casual side, you should be able to find something suitable for your taste of the day.

While there are definitely dozens of possible restaurants you can check out in the city, we'll try to confine our listing to just the top 5 to fit your quite possibly limited schedule. Here are the top restaurants you should definitely check out:

Vincents

Location: Elizabetes iela 19, Riga, LV-1010
Official Website: http://www.restorans.lv/en/

Vincents isn't just popular in Riga but in the whole of Latvia and beyond. It's actually one of the best gourmet places in Northern Europe, which is why it's often packed – especially during the tourist season. If you have every intention of visiting Vincents, then you'd want to schedule ahead or at least be in Riga during the off-peak season so you're guaranteed a table.

A Little Background

Vincents was founded in 1994 and has since grown to become one of the top gourmet establishments in the area. It's actually so popular that it served several distinctive personalities such as Elton John, Prince Charles, and even the Emperor of Japan. Its location also adds to its allure as it is just 15 minutes away from the Old City on foot. From your seat, you can get a beautiful view of Riga while happily savoring your ordered cuisine. The restaurant also plays host to multiple occasions such as birthdays and weddings.

The Food

Another plus of Vincents is the fact that they're strongly associated with local farmers. Many of their dishes are made from organic and freshly harvested ingredients – which means that you'll be getting the best of the best when it comes to taste. The menu of Vincents changes from time to time, depending on what fruits and vegetables are in season. This means that you'll be getting fruits picked at the height of their ripeness and freshness instead of something that's been coaxed into ripening.

The restaurant also features a wine list selected by Sommelier Raimonds Tomsons which you can download from their official site if you want to choose ahead of time. Some of the more popular dishes include Vincent's Canard A La Presse which is prepared right on the table and is good for 2 to 4 persons. There's also the hand-dived sea scallops, and the seared yellow fin tuna in nori leaf served with fresh wasabi, shiitake, and yuzu sauce.

EQUUS

Location: Jēkaba iela 24, Rīga, LV-1050
   Official Website: www.equus.lv

If you're looking for something a little cozier with an old-world feel, then you might want to check out Equus. The interiors are historic and when combined with the delicious food servings, it's a fine dining experience not to be missed in Riga, Latvia.

A Little Background

Located in an old building, Equus literally translates to "a horse" using the Latin language. The name hails from the location of the restaurant, which was originally an 18th century building used as a horse's stable. Perhaps one of the most entertaining aspects of the restaurant is the transparency of the food preparation. You can happily watch the chef cook your food in an open kitchen setting.

The Food

The food itself is excellent with choices offering a combination of Scandinavian food and classics from the Latvian culture. International food choices are also available with snacks and delicacies hailing from all over the world, including the amazing Spanish tapas which is a particular favorite in the area. There's also a Tea Deli concept where tea is prepared on your table in a traditional ceremony. Wines are also available with multiple choices to help you find the best one to go with your food.

Restorans 3

Location: Kalēju iela 3, Rīga, LV-1050
   Official Website: restaurant3.lv

When visiting this restaurant, you'd want to be a little careful with the time you drop by. The kind of food they offer may vary depending on what time you arrive. For example, if you visit before 18:00, you can order a la carte items. Starting 18:00 however, you can choose from some of their gourmet meals with offerings that include a Five Course meal, a Seven Course meal and even a Five Course meal, especially for vegetarians.

A Little Background
   They serve mainly modern Latvian flavors in a classically cozy setting. It's a fairly small place with the tables close together – so don't expect lots of privacy when eating here. A conference room is available for private parties if you're going with a bunch of friends. If you're looking for the real Latvian experience with traditional cuisines updated for the modern palette, then this is the one for you. The restaurant is primarily famous for its fish cuisine with the gourmet cooks staying true to their motto of offering clients a taste of nature.

The Food

Ingredients used for the food are primarily organic and natural. These gourmets serve dishes based on the availability of the ingredients, so some of the items on the menu may not be available due to being off season. On the plus side however, this means that anything you order will be at the peak of ripeness because they're being served when they're at their best.

COD Robata Grill Bar

Location: Tērbatas iela 45, Rīga, LV-1011

Official Website: www.cod.lv

The first ever robata grill in the whole of Latvia, COD is primarily famous for their authentic Japanese cuisine. Now you'd probably ask – why would you go to Latvia if you're just going to eat Japanese food? You'll have to remember that everything in Riga is prepared with a unique twist from the locals. Contemporary additions have been made, but without losing the essence of Japanese cooking with the help of the robata grill.

A Little Background

The restaurant doesn't just promote Japanese cooking. It also showcases the simplicity of the Eastern culture through its interior design. Purity is promoted all through the décor as customers get a quiet blend of clean lines and subtle details. Wooden materials add a very cozy and classic feel to the overall design, allowing you to focus more on the food instead of being overwhelmed by the general surroundings. The result is a more satisfying dining experience with each bite. Note that the restaurant is closed on Sundays, but you can place a reservation for any other day of the week through their official website.

The Food

As mentioned, COD offers primarily Japanese cuisine with a modern twist for the contemporary customer. To complement the robata grilled dishes are Japanese-inspired cocktails or straight up sake or rice wine. Food is prepared using traditional cooking methods of the Japanese with a serving repertoire worthy of any Michelin Star restaurant.

Muusu

Location: Skārņu iela 6, Rīga, LV-1050
Official website: www.muusu.lv

Featuring a Nordic interior with raw brick walls, wood, and linen fabric covering the restaurant – Muusu is the place you want to be for an authentic Riga experience. The restaurant embodies beauty and comfort in one convenient style – combined with an amazing array of food options.

A Little Background

Muusu is proud of its head chef Kaspars Jansons who is one of the best in the city. Through his artistic flair, Jansons promotes dishes that are primarily local in origin. Contemporary Europe can be tasted with every, bite while making sure that all the ingredients used are fresh and natural. Like many restaurants in this list, Muusu takes into consideration the seasons when offering dishes, therefore making sure that everything served on your plate is fresh and at its peak of deliciousness. Due to its popularity, it's best to reserve a table through their website.

The Food

Taking into consideration the local goods and seasonal accents, the Muusu menu may vary from time to time. They offer all kinds of meat from beef, chicken, and lamb to game meat. They have a lamb chop w/ rib served w/ garlic-roasted aubergine puree, peppermint yoghurt sauce, black garlic & red wine broth sauce, and salt-fried celery root. Ask the waiter and you can experience their game meat that's served with wheat grains, oven-baked onion, wild berry puree, wild mushroom pie, and Madeira sage broth sauce.

Riga Fish Market

6

Best Famous Landmarks in the City

Just like Singapore's famous lion – it's practically mandatory to take a picture in one of Riga's landmarks when you visit there. With so many landmarks to choose from, however - which one should you visit first? Here are the top 5 locations in Riga that are uniquely Latvian and should be part of your visit.

House of Blackheads

The House of Blackheads is an address all in itself. There's really no need to specify its location because any local can point you to its general direction. The House of Blackheads is a massive piece of architecture originally built in 1334. It was destroyed during World War II but was eventually rebuilt in 1999.

The House of Blackheads was an elaborate function room of its time when people threw amazing parties with lavish food, music, and dancing. It was originally built for what was known as the Brotherhood of Blackheads composed for unmarried ship owners, foreigners, and merchants of Riga. The House displays different arts, crystal chandeliers, painted ceilings, and even furniture from the 19th century. There are even portraits, snuffboxes, and weapons showcasing the coats and arms of the Blackheads. Even now, the House of Blackheads plays host to several festivities, giving you a glimpse of how it was used in the days when merchants and ship owners had extravagant lifestyles.

Cat House

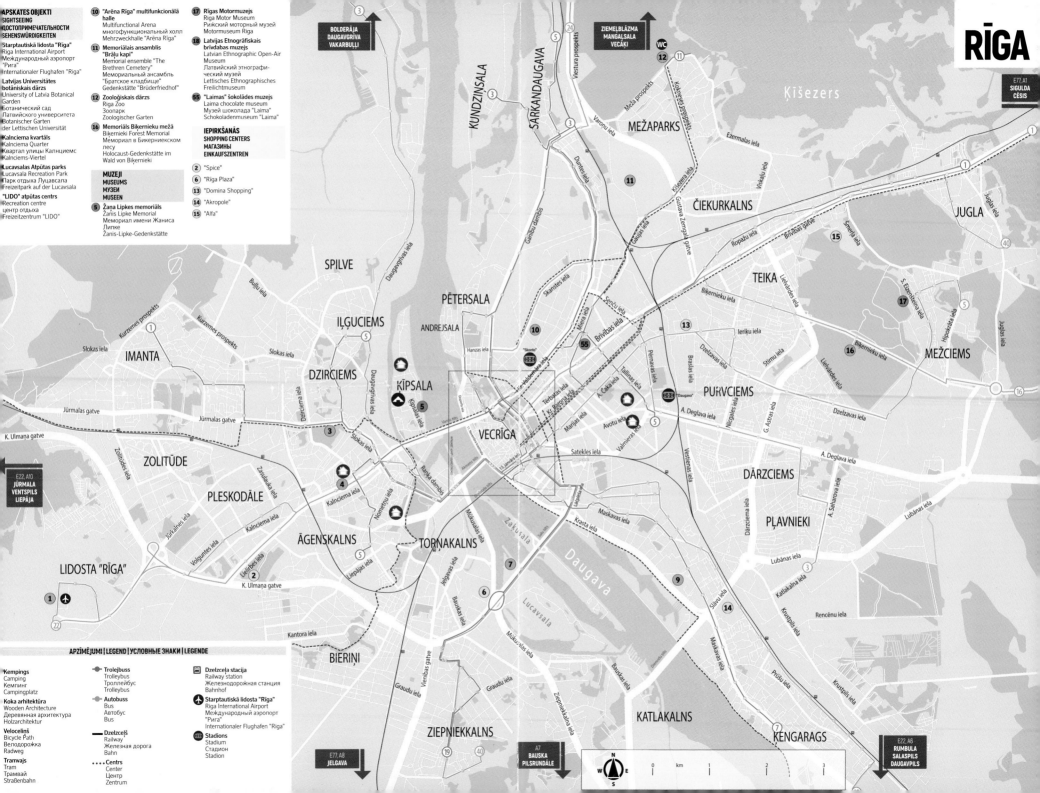

RĪGA

APSKATES OBJEKTI
SIGHTSEEING
ДОСТОПРИМЕЧАТЕЛЬНОСТИ
SEHENSWÜRDIGKEITEN

Starptautiskā lidosta "Rīga"
Riga International Airport
Международный аэропорт "Рига"
Internationaler Flughafen "Riga"

Latvijas Universitātes botāniskais dārzs
University of Latvia Botanical Garden
Ботанический сад Латвийского университета
Botanischer Garten der Lettischen Universität

Kalnciema kvartāls
Kalnciema Quarter
Квартал улицы Калнциемс
Kalnciems-Viertel

Lucavsalas Atpūtas parks
Lucavsala Recreation Park
Парк отдыха Луцавсала
Freizeitpark auf der Lucavsala

"LIDO" atpūtas centrs
Recreation centre
центр отдыха
Freizeitzentrum "LIDO"

10 **"Arēna Rīga" multifunkcionālā halle**
Multifunctional Arena
многофункциональный холл
Mehrzweckhalle "Arēna Rīga"

11 **Memoriālais ansamblis "Brāļu kapi"**
Memorial ensemble "The Brethren Cemetery"
Мемориальный ансамбль "Братское кладбище"
Gedenkstätte "Brüderfriedhof"

12 **Zooloģiskais dārzs**
Riga Zoo
Зоопарк
Zoologischer Garten

16 **Memoriāls Biķernieku mežā**
Biķernieki Forest Memorial
Мемориал в Биķерниекском лесу
Holocaust-Gedenkstätte im Wald von Biķernieki

MUZEJI
MUSEUMS
МУЗЕИ
MUSEEN

5 **Žaņa Lipkes memoriāls**
Žanis Lipke Memorial
Мемориал имени Жаниса Липке
Žanis-Lipke-Gedenkstätte

17 **Rīgas Motormuzejs**
Riga Motor Museum
Рижский моторный музей
Motormuseum Riga

18 **Latvijas Etnogrāfiskais brīvdabas muzejs**
Latvian Ethnographic Open-Air Museum
Латвийский этнографический музей
Lettisches Ethnographisches Freilichtmuseum

55 **"Laimas" šokolādes muzejs**
Laima chocolate museum
Музей шоколада "Laima"
Schokoladenmuseum "Laima"

IEPIRKŠANĀS
SHOPPING CENTERS
МАГАЗИНЫ
EINKAUFSZENTREN

2 "Spice"
6 "Rīga Plaza"
13 "Domina Shopping"
14 "Akropole"
15 "Alfa"

APZĪMĒJUMI | LEGEND | УСЛОВНЫЕ ЗНАКИ | LEGENDE

Kempings
Camping
Кемпинг
Campingplatz

Koka arhitektūra
Wooden Architecture
Деревянная архитектура
Holzarchitektur

Velaceliņš
Bicycle Path
Велодорожка
Radweg

Tramvajs
Tram
Трамвай
Straßenbahn

Trolejbuss
Trolleybus
Троллейбус
Trolleybus

Autobuss
Bus
Автобус
Bus

Dzelzceļš
Railway
Железная дорога
Bahn

Centrs
Center
Центр
Zentrum

Dzelzceļa stacija
Railway station
Железнодорожная станция
Bahnhof

Starptautiskā lidosta "Rīga"
Riga International Airport
Международный аэропорт "Рига"
Internationaler Flughafen "Riga"

Stadions
Stadium
Стадион
Stadion

SKATES OBJEKTI
TSEEING
СТОПРИМЕЧАТЕЛЬНОСТИ
ENSWÜRDIGKEITEN

Rīgas pils
Riga Castle
Рижский замок
Rigaer Schloss

Lielais Kristaps
Great Kristaps
Большой Кристап
Großer Christophorus

Zviedru vārti
Swedish Gate
Шведские ворота
Schwedentor

Svētā Jēkaba katedrāle
St. Jacobs Cathedral
Церковь Св. Иакова
St. Jakob-Kathedrale

"Trīs brāļi"
The Three Brothers
"Три брата"
Die Drei Brüder

Doma luterāņu baznīca
Dome Cathedral
Домский собор
Rigaer Dom

Melngalvju nams
House of Blackheads
Дом Черноголовых
Schwarzhäupterhaus

Pulvertornis
The Powder Tower
Пороховая башня
Pulverturm

Kaķu nams
The Cat House
Кошкин дом
Katzenhaus

Lielā Ģilde
The Great Guild
Большая гильдия
Die Große Gilde

Mazā Ģilde
The Small Guild
Малая гильдия
Die Kleine Gilde

Konventa sēta
Convent Yard
Двор Конвента
Konventhof

Svētā Jāņa baznīca
St. John's Church
Церковь Св. Иоанна
St. Johannes-Kirche

Sinagoga
Riga Synagogue
Рижская синагога
Rigaer Synagoge

Brīvības piemineklis
The Freedom Monument
Памятник Свободы
Das Freiheitsdenkmal

"Laimas" pulkstenis
Laima Clock
Часы Лайма
Laima-Uhr

Latvijas Nacionālā opera
Latvian National Opera
Латвийская национальная опера
Lettische Nationaloper

Latvijas Nacionālā bibliotēka
National Library of Latvia
Латвийская национальная библиотека
Lettische Nationalbibliothek

Pasažieru osta
Passenger Port
Пассажирский порт
Passagierhafen

Jūgendstila kvartāls
The Art Nouveau Quarter
Квартал югендстиля
Jugendstil-Viertel

36 **Kristus Piedzimšanas pareizticīgo katedrāle**
Nativity of Christ Cathedral
Кафедральный собор
Рождества Христова
Christi-Geburt-Kathedrale

38 **Veca Sv. Ģertrūdes baznīca**
Old St. Ģertrude's Church
Старая Гертрудинская церковь
Alte St. Gertrude-Kirche

41 **"Splendid Palace"**
Kinoteātris
Cinema
Кино
Kino

42 **"Saktas ziedu" tirgus**
Sakta Flower Market
Цветочный рынок "Сакта"
Blumenmarkt Sakta

47 **Centrālā dzelzceļa stacija**
Central Railway Station
Центральный вокзал
Hauptbahnhof

49 **Starptautiskā autoosta**
International Coach Terminal
Международный автовокзал
Internationaler Busbahnhof

50 **Centrāltirgus**
Central Market
Центральный рынок
Zentralmarkt

51 **Spīķeru kvartāls**
Spīķeri Quarter
Квартал Спīķери
Speicherviertel

MUZEJI
MUSEUMS
МУЗЕИ
MUSEEN

3 **LNMM izstāžu zāle "Arsenāls"**
Arsenāls Exhibition Space
Выставочный зал "Арсенал"
Ausstellungssaal Arsenāls

7 **Mākslas muzejs "Rīgas Birža"**
Art Museum Riga Bourse
Художественный музей "Рижская биржа"
Kunstmuseum Rigaer Börse

9 **Rīgas vēstures un kuģniecības muzejs**
Museum of the History of Riga and Navigation
Музей истории Риги и мореходства
Rigaer Museum für Geschichte und Schifffahrt

10 **1991. gada barikāžu muzejs**
1991 Barricades Museum
Музей баррикад 1991-ого года
Barrikadenmuseum

11 **"Rīgas mākslas telpa"**
Riga Art Space
Художественное пространство Риги
Kunstraum Riga

14 **Mencendorfa nams**
Mentzendorff House
Дом Менцендорфа
Mentzendorff-Haus

15 **Latvijas Kara muzejs**
Latvian War Museum
Латвийский военный музей
Lettisches Kriegsmuseum

20 **Dekoratīvās mākslas un dizaina muzejs**
Riga Museum of Decorative Arts and Design
Музей декоративного искусства и дизайна
Museum für dekorative Kunst und Design

22 **Rīgas Porcelāna muzejs**
Riga Porcelain Museum
Рижский музей фарфора
Rigaer Porzellanmuseum

31 **Rīgas Jūgendstila muzejs**
Art Nouveau Museum
Рижский музей югендстиля
Jugendstilmuseum Riga

33 **P. Stradiņa Medicīnas vēstures muzejs**
P. Stradins Museum of the History of Medicine
Музей истории медицины им. П. Страдыня
P. Stradiņ Medizinhistorisches Museum

34 **Latvijas Nacionālais mākslas muzejs (LNMM)**
Latvian National Museum of Art
Латвийский национальный художественный музей
Lettisches Nationales Kunstmuseum

35 **Latvijas Okupācijas muzejs**
Museum of the Occupation of Latvia 1940-1991
Музей оккупации Латвии
Lettisches Okkupationsmuseum

37 **Ebreji Latvijā**
Jews In Latvia
Евреи в Латвии
Juden in Lettland

39 **KGB Stūra māja**
Former KGB Headquarters
КГБ Угловой дом
KGB Das Eckhaus

43 **Latvijas Nacionālais vēstures muzejs**
National History Museum of Latvia
Национальный музей истории Латвии
Lettisches Nationalmuseum für Geschichte

44 **Latvijas Dabas muzejs**
Natural History Museum of Latvia
Латвийский музей природы
Lettisches Naturkundemuseum

52 **Rīgas geto un Latvijas Holokausta muzejs**
Riga Ghetto and Latvian Holocaust Museum
Музей рижского гетто и Холокоста в Латвии
Rigaer Ghetto und Lettisches Holocaustmuseum

53 **Latvijas Fotogrāfijas muzejs**
Latvian Museum of Photography
Латвийский музей фотографии
Lettisches Museum für Fotografie

54 **Modes muzejs**
Fashion Museum
Музей моды
Modemuseum

SKATU LAUKUMI
VIEWING PLATFORMS
СМОТРОВЫЕ ПЛОЩАДКИ
AUSSICHTSPUNKTE

12 **Sv. Pētera luterāņu baznīca**
St. Peter's Church
Церковь Святого Петра
St. Petri-Kirche

53 **Latvijas Zinātņu akadēmija**
Latvian Academy of Sciences
Латвийская академия наук
Akademie der Wissenschaften

IEPIRKŠANĀS
SHOPPING CENTERS
МАГАЗИНЫ
EINKAUFSZENTREN

28 "Galerija Centrs"

40 "Galleria Riga"

45 "Berga Bazārs"

46 "Origo"

48 "Stockmann"

APZĪMĒJUMI | LEGEND | УСЛОВНЫЕ ЗНАКИ | LEGENDE

Veloceliņš
Bicycle Path
Велодорожка
Radweg

Tramvajs
Tram
Трамвай
Straßenbahn

Trolejbuss
Trolleybus
Троллейбус
Trolleybus

Autobuss
Bus
Автобус
Bus

Rīgas Tūrisma informācijas centrs
Riga Tourist Information Centre
Рижский Туристический информационный центр
Rigaer Tourismus-Informationszentrum

Kuģīšu piestātne
Boat dock
Причал
Bootsanlegestelle

Starptautiskā lidosta "Rīga"
Riga International Airport
Международный аэропорт "Рига"
Internationaler Flughafen "Riga"

RĪGA
CENTRS
CENTER
ЦЕНТР
ZENTRUM

If you love cats, this is definitely one of the top places to visit. Don't be disappointed though if you don't see any cats inside the building. The Cat House was named such because of the two angry cats placed on the turrets rooftops of the building. There are two versions as to why this architectural design was done. The first version is that this was done out of anger against the house of the Great Guild which directly faced the Cat House.

Accordingly, the people who commissioned the Cat House were refused membership with the Great Guild. The second version is that it was done in defiance of the Riga City Council after a dispute. The Riga City Council was erected on the same side as the Great Guild but was eventually destroyed. In any case, the Cat House is a wonderful example of medieval architecture with bits and pieces of new art.

Livu Square

The Livu Square may be defined as the heart of the heart of the city.

Simply put, it's the town square and like all squares, it is surrounded by numerous restaurants, beautiful huts, outdoor cafes, and even residential buildings.

It's a great place to just sit back and people watch as everyone else goes about their day. If you want to see what Riga really looks like from the viewpoint of someone who lives there, then this is the place you want to visit.

Jauniela

Jauniela is actually a road that's best viewed on foot. It forms part of the Old Town and features some of the most amazing architecture of old buildings.

If you're interested in checking out building facades, then this is the kind of walk you want to be in, each apartment-style building having the kind of exterior that's obviously been designed with heart. If you're taking the Old Town walking tour, there's no way you can miss Jauniela.

St. Savior's Church

Finally, there's the St. Savior's Church which is just one of the many churches found in Riga city. This is an Anglican Church close to the Riga Castle and the Daugava River. The foundation stone of the church was placed in 1857 and continued to stand during the Soviet occupation. Today, the church has a dual purpose as it operates a soup kitchen for the homeless of Latvia and a club for elderly people.

Obviously, that's just a very small amount of landmarks in Latvia so even as you make sure that you visit these places, don't forget to take note of the sites also listed in this book.

7

Best Museums, Theatres and Art Galleries

Latvian culture is definitely worth exploring, and most of the prominent aspects of their culture can be found in the capital city of Riga. If you're looking for culture, these are the places you want to visit:

Best Museums in Riga

Musee Art Nouveau
   Location: Alberta iela 12, Riga 1010, Latvia

Don't be confused as this museum also goes by the name of Maxim's Art Nouveau "Collection of 1900". It's a private collection of new art which originated from the private collection of Pierre Cardin. He was the owner of Maxim's restaurant since the year 1981, said restaurant being the main symbol for art nouveau in Riga. He of which have been signed by their creators.

Covering a span of 12 rooms, these artworks are displayed in a building which is now classified as a historic monument in Latvia. Perhaps the most prominent pieces in attendance are those inspired by Antoni Gaudi, furniture by Majorelle, and even recreations of bedrooms from the 1900s time period. Guided tours are available for the museums on a daily basis except for Monday and Tuesday.

National History Museum of Latvia
    Location: Brivibas bulvaris 32, Riga 1050, Latvia

Founded in 1869, your vacation to Latvia is not complete without checking out at least this museum. It was established by the Riga Latvian Society with the mission to collect, preserve, research, & popularize spiritual as well as material culture from Latvia & the world from the ancient times until today. The museum has had many homes in the past with the artworks being moved from one place to another.

The Three Brothers
    Location: Maza Pils St 17, 19, 21, Riga 1050, Latvia

The Three Brothers got its name from the simple fact that is composed of three houses sitting side by side. Taken together, they're actually the oldest dwelling houses in Riga and they represent various periods of dwelling architectural development in the city.

If you visit the Three Brothers, you'll also be visiting the Latvian Museum of Architecture.

Latvian National Museum of Art
   Location: 1 Janis Rozentals Square, Riga 1010, Latvia

As the name suggests, this is the national museum and therefore displays some of the most treasured cultural pieces of the country.

It is home to more than 52,000 works of art that showcase the development of Latvian culture starting with the middle of the 18th century. Built in 1905, the building itself is fairly hard to miss as it's one of the most impressive in the area. The same building was the first one built with the intention of turning it into a museum.

International Museum of Vodka
   Location: Kri jana Barona iela 136f, Riga 1012, Latvia

You read it right – this is a museum dedicated solely to vodka. On the plus side, you're going to get the experience of a lifetime with this trip. On the downside however, you just can't walk inside the museum and expect a tour. All tours have to be booked and pre-arranged. Otherwise, you might be refused entry. The museum is 100% independent and private – but the contents are all vodka-related and every bit as interesting.

Art Galleries

Art Museum Riga Bourse

A gallery and museum in one, this place is situated in the heart of Riga and occupies a 19th century building.

It displays 16th and 19th century paintings as well as European porcelain from the 18th to 20th century.

Riga Art Space

Containing contemporary art exhibitions as well as live music, this beautiful museum boasts of a central location that's easy to visit by modern art lovers. The gallery is fairly new as it opened only in 2008 but already has an excellent array of works from both local and international artists.

Happy Art Museum

The name is a dead giveaway – but that doesn't mean you should skip it. The Happy Art Museum is dedicated towards contemporary works with a mind towards showcasing modern artist exhibitions and collecting its own permanent collection. They have paintings, sculptures, and graphics – all arranged in a one-of-a-kind setup that engages people to walk around and enjoy. The gallery welcomes the hosting of corporate events, seminars, performances, film forums and others.

Putti

First opening its doors in 2009, the Putti Art Gallery is focused towards showcasing contemporary jewelry of Latvia. They also display international works, but it is the local designs that get the most spotlight. Hand-crafted jewels are displayed at their best advantage made by graduates of Estonian and Latvian academies.

Jurmala Open Air Museum

Definitely offering something different, the Jurmala Open Air Museum is located outdoors – hence the name. The museum is free and showcases the fishing history of Latvia, allowing tourists to find out exactly how fishermen used to live in these little wooden houses.

Best Theatres

Riga, Latvia is home to several theatres, each one more beautiful than the next. Being part of the EU, this Baltic state is more than ready to compete with the likes of Paris when it comes to cultural assets. Here are the top 5 theatres you should definitely visit when in Riga.

Latvian National Opera which was founded as early as 1918. It shows all opera masterpieces as well as a ballet troupe that performs on a regular basis.

The New Riga Theatre is the newest theatre in the city, having been founded in 1992. It's a beautiful piece of work with an offering of shows more focused on modern performances catering towards a socially active set of audience.

The Latvian State Puppet Theatre was started in 1944 and it's an excellent option if you're visiting Riga as a family. As the name suggests, the puppet show is extremely attractive for children and should be equally entertaining for the adults.

Dailes Theatre deserves a spot in this list for the simple reason that it focuses on modern foreign plays. Established in 1920, it's one of the most successful theatres in the country.

Mikhail Checkhov Riga Russian Theatre is the oldest theatre in the country, established as far back as 1883. This makes the theatre a favorite for the lover of the classics as this professional drama theatre showcases classical plays with a dab of experimental performances on a routine basis. If you check with their official website, you'll find that they also frequently show the work of foreign playwrights.

8

Best Coffee Shops

If you're looking for a spot where you can just sit down and chill without eating anything heavy, you can check out the many coffee shops available in Riga. Even with just coffee as their main product, you'll find that many of these coffee shops have a personality of their own that you can't help but love. Following are the top coffee shops in the city according to visitors.

Radisson Blue

Location: Elizabetes iela 55, Rīga, LV-1010, Latvia

Known for their excellent customer service, the location of Radisson Blue makes it incredibly easy to find wherever you happen to be staying. It's smack in the heart of the city, but beautifully laid back so that you can truly relax in one of their comfortable seats. Unlike most of the coffee shops today, Radisson Blue is not blaring a series of hard music on the speakers but instead maintains a quiet atmosphere, perfect for working or sitting quietly with a good friend. After a leisurely sightseeing trip for the day, Radisson Blue is the most convenient spot you can go to for a dash of invigorating coffee.

Innocent Café

Location: Blaumaņa ielā 34-1a, Rīgā, LV-1011

Innocent Café is not as innocent as you'd expect since this buzzing spot in Riga also serves wine. That's right, you have the choice between all sorts of coffee and if you get tired from all the caffeine, you can switch it up to wine. This makes it possible for you to stay here for long periods of time, just tapping on your laptop or watching the people pass by. It's actually a highly popular cafe with people moving in and out on a routine basis. Even the locals go to Innocent, which is a testimony to just how special the spot can be. If you get hungry, they're also famous for their burgers, while fancy cakes also wait your delectation.

Miit

Location: Lāčplēša iela 10, Rīga, LV-1010, Latvia

A haven for hipsters, the Miit was originally a bicycle workshop that evolved into one of the most popular spots for vegetarians. They serve excellent strong coffee with several variations for those who prefer something slightly weaker and with a whole lot more of sugar. The vegetarian delicacies are really one of the many reasons why people visit Miit, not to mention their endless choices of cheesecakes. As a nod to the original use of the building, this coffee shop is lined with bicycles and bicycle parts as the main décor, creating a very garage-feel to the whole ensemble. If you're hankering for meat, the coffee shop also serves non-vegetarian dishes for their breakfast.

Index Café

Location: 17a Lielirbes str., *Riga* / Panorama Plaza

A popular coffee place, Index Café also serves all kinds of food items and have them available for delivery. They're big on keeping healthy servings, so if you're on a diet while on vacation, this is definitely the place you want to visit. Index Café is decidedly modern with an exterior that seems plain, but come inside and you'll instantly be welcomed by the amazing smell of delicious food items. Aside from the delicious coffee mixes of hot and cold drinks, you can also choose to eat burgers, sandwiches, canapés, burgers, noodles, and desserts. They even have freshly squeezed juices if you're looking for something light and sweet.

Bufete Gauja

Location: Stabu iela 32, Centra rajons, Rīga, LV-1011, Latvia

If you want to eat in the middle of Riga during the Soviet era, this is the coffee shop for you. The whole place is designed with Soviet era articles so that you can chill out in a perfect recreation of the past. If you think this is going to be a gloomy situation with all blacks and browns however, you're in for a surprise. The color combinations are a perfect blend of brightness and wooden classics – allowing for comfort without causing boredom.

Board games and magazines – all from the 70s – litter the area, letting you find out exactly what's on the front page in the days your parents were still young and single. The food however, is far from being a holdover from the past as Bufete Gauja prepares their coffee only with the most modern machines, pressing that caffeine down to its very last drop. You have the choice of getting something dark and bitter or perhaps something with more sugar than your body can handle. Even the locals come to this place for some much needed rest and relaxation.

9

Top Bars and Night Clubs

The capital of Latvia, Riga is far from the quiet and sedate city you seem to think. While daytime gives you the chance to walk around and enjoy relative solitude, the night time lets you meet all the movers and shakers of the city. That's right – Riga is home to several bars and nightclubs, each one having their own "thing" to keep the customers happy and entertained. Here are the best five of the bars and nightclubs in the city.

Best Bars in Riga

I Love You Bar
   Location: *9 Aldaru ielā, Riga, Latvia*

This bar's name is definitely memorable and the bar itself is even more so. Not surprisingly, the I Love You bar is the most popular one in Riga with a cozy feel to it, thanks mainly to the plushy couches. The music varies from time to time as DJ's come and go, giving you their own kind of music to go with the many types of drinks available in their closet. The bar actually has their own small record label so if you're looking for brand new music, this is a great place to check out. It's not hard to find this bar because it's close to the Swedish Gate with an old-stone world feel to it that's sturdy, deep, and old-school. The I Love You bar gives an impression that it's been here for ages and will continue to do so.

Skyline Bar
   Location: *55 Elizabetes iela, Riga, Latvia*

The Skyline Bar is located in the famous Radisson Blue hotel, which makes it a very convenient place to visit if you happen to stay in the same hotel. It's considered to be one of the best in Riga, which is probably why the cocktail prices are a little bit on the expensive side. Are they worth it though? Of course – the general ambience, the quality of the customers, and the food are well worth going for. With Radisson Blue located in the Old Town, it's also an excellent place to chill out after checking out the numerous sights and sounds of the old city. Nearby is also the Art Nouveau District, which should spark some much needed creativity on your side. Note that the bar can be quite busy, so if you want this in your itinerary, you better come during the off peak season.

Rock Café
    Location: 2/4 Mārstaļu ielā, Riga, Latvia

No – this is not the Hard Rock Café because it's so much better with its unique feel. The Rock Café is located in the Old Town district and features a dance floor where you and your friends can jam out to a variety of music. They even have live concerts on certain days if you feel like getting some unique sounds for the night. There's a host of possible entertaining features in the Rock Café including a pool room and some karaoke where you can choose to sing from thousands of possible songs. Catering to a lively bunch of people, the Rock Café isn't a place where you can just sit down and quietly drink beer. The place is lively and jumping with energy, especially during a Saturday night. Catering mainly to the young adult crowd, you'll have no problem meeting new faces and chatting to people while drinking finely crafted beer and other cocktail options.

Aussie Backpackers Pub
    Location: 43 Vaļņu iela, Riga, Latvia

As the name suggests, this is an Australian pub located in Riga, Latvia. If you're from the country Down Under, then this will be a little bit of home during your vacation in Europe. This down to Earth pub is located near the Riga Old Town Hostel, which is why it's always packed by tourists and expats looking for a little bit of home in a foreign country. It's actually a fairly big pub because it's spread over three floors, each one packed with people looking for a taste of Australia. They won't be disappointed as the craft brew here are decidedly Australian in origin, not to mention the general motif of the décor. Drinking games are also celebrated within the club and the atmosphere is one of friendly revelry.

Kanepes Kulturas Centrs
  Location: 15 Skolas iela, Riga, Latvia

Last in this Top 5 list is the Kanepes Kulturas, which is a bar and a cultural hub all at the same time. That's probably fairly obvious based on the name of the bar – but you'll really understand the complexity of the name once you drop by for a visit. If you're a fan of art and love to check out the local offerings, then this is the place to be. Everyone in the pub are just as interested in art as you are so you'll have no problem finding like-minded people in the area. For entertainment, the bar offers experimental live music and even film screenings. Close by is the Art Nouveau District which still has traces of the Baltic German and Russian occupation.

Best Night Clubs in Riga

Skyline Bar

Perched atop the famous Radisson Blue Hotel, the Skyline Bar has an entrance fee of just 3 Euros and is packed on a nightly basis. It's well worth it though, as the cocktails and the people give you the time of your life.

Labais Krasts

A nightlife experience is never complete without at least checking out the beer gardens. You can escape the busy tourist-bars and choose to go where the locals go – to Labais Krasts where the cocktails are swapped for cheap but quality ales.

B Bars

You might regret it in the morning – but if you don't taste the Riga

Black Balsam, then you're going to regret it for the rest of your life. This dangerous drink is served at B Bars and is classified as 90% proof. It contains more than two dozen plants combined with vodka. Make sure to have someone with you when you take a swig.

Pulkvedim Neviens Neraksta

A mouthful of a name, the words actually translate to "Nobody Writes to the Colonel" which can but puzzling unless you know the backstory. It's actually after a written novella by Gabriel Garcia Marquez, the bar itself being a home to alternative music fans. During the early afternoons, it functions as a bar but later turns into a nightclub.

Riga Pub Crawl

If you're not the kind of person who loves to stay in one nightclub during the night, you might want to take the Riga Pub Crawl. It's essentially a walking tour of the Riga nightlife with a guide that helps you jump from one club to the next in a never ending night adventure. This way, you'll hit the best spots in just one go.

10

Special Things You Can Only Do in Riga

So what exactly has Riga to offer its visitors? Here are some of the activities you can only do in this beautiful city. To keep this book as extensive as possible however, we're removing from the list those activities or places that we're already mentioned in the previous

Chapters.

Old Town Walking Tour

Every tourist in Riga takes the walking tour around the Old Town – and for a very good reason. The Old Town is representative of everything Riga and Latvia. For example, the mouth of Daugava River dates as far back as 1201 which means that you'll be seeing lots of stuff way older than the Soviet Era. The great thing here is that the Old Town is very pedestrian-friendly so you'll have no problem exploring the area without having to spend a single cent. A relatively safe space with a low crime rate, there's not much to worry about as long as you do most of your walking in the morning. With weather that's more on the cool side, there's no need to worry about the heat drying out your skin.

The walking tours are offered on a routine basis and usually covers around 1.5 hours of your time. You can do the walk by yourself for free but the guided tour will give you so much more information to chew on.

Plus, you'll be in the company of other tourists, which should be fun! If your time is limited in Riga, the guided tour will make sure you hit all the prominent spots of the Old Town.

Go Shopping at the Central Market

Every city's market is similar but different in that you'll be getting something that's uniquely that of the City. For Riga, the Central Market is considered to be one of the most advanced marketplaces in Europe. It's also one of the largest, accommodating as many as 100,000 people on any given day. You can spend hours just walking around the Central Market and you'll definitely find more than a dozen things you'd want to buy. The word "Central' is true to form because it's close to the Daugava River, just next to the Riga International Bus Terminal and the Central Railway Station. Hence, even if you're not staying close to the Old Town, you'll have no problem visiting this haven of a marketplace.

The original building was built in the 1920s, this Central Marketplace plays host to numerous products from fresh fruits, vegetables, meat, ready to eat products, packaged products, souvenir products, and so much more. The size of the place isn't really surprising considering how it was originally used as a hangar for military airships. You'll be glad to know that visiting the Central Market also means you'll be steeping in a UNESCO World Heritage site.

Admire the Art Nouveau Section

The Old Town and the Art Nouveau Section are close to each other, allowing you to seamlessly move from one portion to the next in an endless series of excellent architecture. So what makes the Art Nouveau stand out from the medieval buildings?

The Art Nouveau or "new art" is famous for the simple fact that they were built during the economic boom of the 19th and 20th centuries. As a result, you get splendidly built buildings commissioned by people who had the means to make them as spectacular as possible. Usually consisting of several floors, the Art Nouveau Architecture is done in long and tall designs with intricate patterns. There's never two similar buildings, which means that every stop you make is unique.

Around 1/3 of the architecture in Riga are classified as Art Nouveau, so you might find yourself spending hours and hours exploring the area, perhaps getting a shot with each one for your social media account. With an excellent background, you'll find that every picture will be worthy of an Instagram post. Located in what is known as the "quiet center" of Riga, you'll have no problem finding these eye-catching buildings and there will be no loss of picture-worthy locations, even during the tourist season. Streets to check out are the Elizabetes, Vilandes, Alberta, and Rupniecibas.

St. Peter's Church

This church went through several constructions, which is why it has such an imposing edifice as several minds went into building this amazing structure.

The first mention of the church was in 1209 but it continued to be built during the Gothic, Romanesque, and Baroque periods. Perhaps one of the best things about the church is the panoramic view of the city, perfect for watching the sunrise or the sunset.

Panorama Observation Deck

A bird's eye view of the city can be fully appreciated through the Observation Deck. The name "Panorama" is as honest as it gets because absolutely nothing obstructs the view. You can do a full 360 degree circle and see the totality of the city. The terrace is big enough that large groups can come to the place and see what they're visiting from such a high vantage point. For couples, this might well be the most romantic point in Latvia.

Vermanes Park

Covering a total of 5 hectares, the Vermanes Park is the oldest public garden in Riga. It contains exotic trees, a rose garden, and a restaurant where you can eat after walking through the lush greeneries. A granite obelisk stands in the heart of the Park which was made in 1829. Sadly, the obelisk was destroyed before World War II but rebuilt in 2000 so what you'll see if fairly new but with an old history. There's also a sundial and fountain installed in the park. While one might argue that the Vermanes Park is just like any other park – you'll have to remember that this park remained intact during the World War II era. It's also an honest depiction of life in Riga as it's a favorite spot for many locals.

Illusions Room Riga

If you're looking for something a little less cultural, then make sure to check out the Illusions Room. It's the kind of place where you'd need lots of space in your mobile phone for pictures because you'd want to take as many as you can! There's the Upside Down Room, the Mirror Maze, the Anti-Gravity Room and so much more.

Bank Job Escape Game

Do you want to test your wits in Riga? Here's a great place to do so! The Bank Job Escape Game lets you play with your mind while at the same time having fun in a controlled atmosphere. It's like being in a real live video game with friends as your team mates. Unfortunately, it's not exactly a cool game if you're alone.

Day Biking Tour

If you want to lose some weight while seeing most of Riga, you can join one of the many biking tours available through tour guides.

You'll be equipped with the best biking material and sweep through the many parks of Riga. It's an up close take on nature and will let you breathe in the cool air – as well as get to know other tourists.

11

3 Days in Riga – Travel Itinerary

So you've booked yourself a 3-day vacation to Riga but still unsure of what to do during those 3 days. As already discussed, Riga is jam packed with welcoming places - nightclubs, bars, restaurants, and activities – so it can be quite tough to make your selection. Still, an attempt must be made so check out the suggested itinerary for your 3-Day Trip. The time you arrive on Riga may vary, but we're guessing that you land in the morning, spend a few hours taking a much needed rest from the trip, and then get your walking your shoes ready for some much needed exploration.

Day 1

Assuming that you arrived in the morning, make sure to first have your lunch in the city before deciding to explore the area. If you arrived from a different time zone, then remember the golden rule when it comes to jet lag – adopt to the time of your current location. Hence, if you arrive in Riga in time for lunch, then you'd better eat that lunch. Exploration can start any time between 1PM to 2PM, which should be just enough time for you to eat and refresh yourself in the hotel room.

Explore Riga

Start your first day by exploring the Old Town. This is a must for your first day in the city, especially if you spent most of the morning sorting out your belongings after arriving in your hotel. By choosing to explore the Old Town on your first day, it becomes so much easier to control your time during the afternoon. As mentioned, a guided tour of the Old Town shouldn't take more than 1.5 hours with a guide giving you a rundown of some of the most important portions of the Old Town.

Since this is the center for almost anything, you shouldn't have a hard time walking around the city. With most hotels located smack in the center of the Old Town, you don't even need to grab a ride in order to check out the old world architecture that this city has to offer. There's no specific stops during your exploration – check out as much as you can, pause in the right places and take as many pictures as you'd want.

Now, there are several places you'd want to check out, but the important landmarks are conveniently located in one pedestrian friendly area. Here are some of the landmarks you should definitely check out on your first day:

· House of Blackheads
· St. Peter's Church
· Liv Square
· Great and Small Guilds
· Cat House

Savor the Coffee – Skyline or Rock Café

At around 3PM or 4PM, make sure to stop by any of the famous coffee shops in Riga. You'll find that there are lots of cafés conveniently located in the Old Town so there's no need to go far. There's the Innocent Café and the Radisson Blue Café, but feel free to check out other places to suit your palate. The coffee will give you an added boost for the rest of the afternoon and most of the night.

Continue with Your Old Town Tour

During your first day, your focus should really be in the Old Town, just

admiring the architecture. There's time to really look inside them the next day but for now, make a note of the location of the following:
- Riga's Dome Cathedral
- St. James Barracks
- Old City Walls
- Swedish Gate
- Riga Castle

Canal and Daugava River

After walking through the Old Town, you'll eventually get to the canal for some much needed rest for your feet. This time, you can take a river cruise through the canal that will eventually lead you to the famous Daugava River. To get here however, you'll have to go to the Bastejkalna Park first which is located near the edge of the Old Town.

Sit by one of the benches and just put your feet up for a few minutes before going to the canal's edge. There's a service there that offers an hour-long boat ride which departs every 30 minutes or so. Hence, you shouldn't have to worry too much if you decide to chill out for the better part of an hour before taking the ride. The cruise should cost around 12 Euros.

See a Show

Make sure to visit at least one of the famous theatres in Riga – preferably the Latvian National Opera. The building in itself is masterful but the shows are a sight to behold. Check out the schedules as soon as you arrive in Riga and make a point of visiting at least once during your stay.

Check Out a Famous Bar – Skyline and Rock Cafe

Come night time, you'd want to find some food, relaxing music, and perhaps the company of people who know the place. What better place to go than a local bar? The Skyline Bar and the Rock Café are just two of the bars you can visit in the Old Town, allowing you to eat and drink without having to go far. Dinner is the first order of the night with perhaps some cocktail drinks to help you sleep tonight. You're probably a little tired so skip the nightclub on your first day – there's plenty of time for that the next day.

Day 2

Your second day in Riga gives you a full 24 hours to explore and hopefully lots of energy to do the exploring. This time, you can go a bit further than the Old Town, possibly visiting famous beaches in the area. Here's what you should check out for the second day:

Jurmala Day Trip

With the Baltic Sea practically a stone's throw away, a day trip to the beach is definitely a must. The Jurmala Day Trip will get you as close to the beach as possible, the sea breeze hitting your face with a clean and invigorating scent. To get to Jurmala, here's what you should know:

- Start from Riga's Central Station, which will take you to Majori. The ride should take around 30 minutes and the cost is around 2.73 Euro, back and forth.
- From Majori, you can take a long walk to the beach. Once you

reach Dzintari, you can walk back, this time taking a different route through the residential area where there's an abundance of wooden villas.

There's an online railway system that should help you figure out when to take the train. Fortunately, the train leaves every 30 minutes so you won't have to wait in between stops.

Visit a Free Museum

Hey, since you're already here – why not stop by the Jurmala Open Air Museum? As mentioned, it's completely free and gives you a glimpse of the past from the viewpoint of a fisherman.

Lunch Near the Art Nouveau

You can spend the better part of several hours in Jurmala just walking around and feeling the breeze. Pretty soon however, you're going to get hungry so better hop onto the train and go back to where you came from. Once you arrive in the Old Town, you can choose to walk a different path and arrive at the Art Nouveau center of the city. The Art Nouveau center is home to some of the most beautiful architectures, built during a time when people can afford such lavish homes. Depending on the time of the day, you can have some food at a nearby café or a full meal at a nearby restaurant.

With the Art Nouveau also a famous tourist walking spot, you'll have no problem checking out a restaurant close by such as Epopey, the Green Tomato Pizzeria, and even the Koala Café which should be great for Australian tourists.

Night Clubbing

Since this is going to be your second night in Riga, you might as well party through the night. Jump through several clubs and bars or perhaps join a tour specifically for bar hopping.

Day 3

Visit the Central Market

Your last day should definitely be dedicated towards souvenir shopping. The Central Market is a must – only just so you can see all the fresh fruits, vegetables, and other merchandise displayed on the stalls. It's unlikely that you'll be able to walk through the central market even if you spend the whole day there, so you might as well reserve shopping for the last day.

Look at the Swedish Gate

The Swedish Gate and the Old City Walls are remnants of a time when the Swedish took the city over. It was built in 1698 and has been preserved even though the rest of the original walls are now gone. Here's a little something for the macabre – the apartment above the gate was owned by the city executioner. The night before he executed a person, he would often put a red rose on his window. Creepy.

Make Sure to Get a Spa

Latvian Spa is something to remember because it's exhaustive, invigorating, and cheap! The service is excellent and you'll feel like a pampered princess by the time you're ready to leave. If you're lucky, your hotel would have an in-house spa but that shouldn't stop you from trying the others!

You should know that there are day tours and half-day tours available for tourists. There are even walking tours and biking tours so if you want your itinerary to be more solid, you can easily arrange things with a guide and have a more streamlined tour of Latvia, Riga within your limited time.

Riga Art Stones

Conclusion

That's it! Your 3 days' vacation in Riga should be as exciting and as stimulating as you want it to be. Note that the information you got from this book may not be as exhaustive as Latvia continues to upgrade their facilities and tourist attractions to give you an awesome experience.

Just remember that no matter when you decide to go – it's always a good idea to plan long and hard so you'll visit all the places you want to check out.

Thank You

Riga Bears

I want to thank you for reading this book! I sincerely hope that you received value from it!

If you received value from this book, I want to ask you for a favour .Would you be kind enough to leave a review for this book on Amazon?

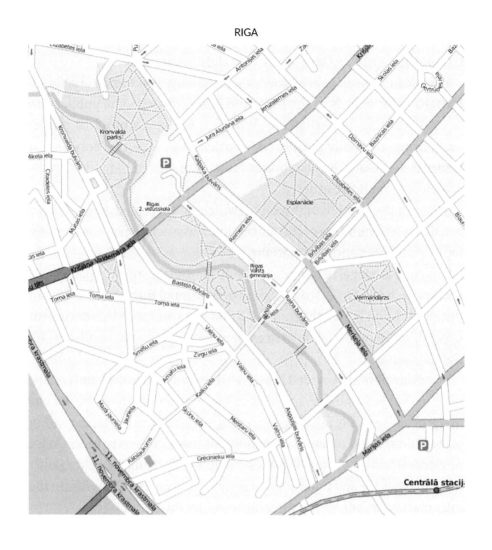

© OpenStreetMap contributors
Credit : https://www.openstreetmap.org/copyright

THANK YOU

95

Printed in Great Britain
by Amazon

26835420R00061